INSIDE THE NFL

NEW YORK JETS

by Charlie Beattie

Abdo & Daughters
MIDDLE GRADE NONFICTION

An imprint of Abdo Publishing
abdobooks.com

ABDOBOOKS.COM

Published by Abdo Publishing, a division of ABDO, PO Box 398166, Minneapolis, Minnesota 55439.

Printed in China.
052025
092025

Cover Photos: Jim McIsaac/Getty Images Sport/Getty Images (Breece Hall); Focus on Sport/Getty Images (Joe Namath)
Interior Photos: Jeff Lewis/AP Images, 4–5; Cooper Neill/Getty Images Sport/Getty Images, 6 (top), 61 (top right); Thearon W. Henderson/Getty Images Sport/Getty Images, 6 (bottom); Nick Cammett/Getty Images Sport/Getty Images, 7 (top), 63; Kirk Irwin/AP Images, 7 (bottom); Elsa/Getty Images Sport/Getty Images, 8, 9, 55; David J. Phillip/AP Images, 10; Abdo Publishing, 12–13, 58; John Lindsay/AP Images, 14–15, 60 (bottom left); Bettmann/Getty Images, 16, 18, 35; New York Daily News Archive/Getty Images, 17; Frank Hurley/New York Daily News Archive/Getty Images, 19; Tony Tomsic/AP Images, 20 (top), 33 (top); Harry Harris/AP Images, 20 (bottom); AP Images, 21, 23 (top), 60 (bottom right); Vernon Biever/AP Images, 22; Focus on Sport/Getty Images Sport/Getty Images, 23 (bottom), 29 (top), 30, 33 (bottom), 36–37, 39 (top), 39 (bottom), 43 (top), 60 (top), 61 (top left); Focus on Sport/Getty Images, 24, 25, 32, 34; Al Messerschmidt Archive/AP Images, 26–27, 47, 50; Corbis/Bettmann Archive/Getty Images, 28; James Drake/Getty Images Sport/Getty Images, 29 (bottom); Peter Read Miller/AP Images, 38; Paul Spinelli/AP Images, 40; Al Messerschmidt/AP Images, 41; James Hughes/New York Daily News Archive/Getty Images, 42; George Gojkovich/Getty Images Sport/Getty Images, 43 (bottom); Al Pereira/Michael Ochs Archives/Getty Images, 44; John T. Greilick/AP Images, 45; Paul Sakuma/AP Images, 46, 61 (bottom); Al Pereira/Getty Images Sport/Getty Images, 48–49; Keith Torrie/New York Daily News Archive/Getty Images, 51; Tom DiPace/AP Images, 52 (top); M. David Leeds/Getty Images Sport/Getty Images, 52 (bottom); Greg Trott/AP Images, 53; Denis Poroy/AP Images, 54 (top); Al Bello/Getty Images Sport/Getty Images, 54 (bottom); Alan Schaefer/Icon Sportswire/Getty Images, 56; Robert Sabo/New York Daily News/Getty Images, 57; Luke Hales/Getty Images Sport/Getty Images, 59

Editor: Arnold Ringstad
Series Designer: Laura Graphenteen
Production Designer: Katharine Hale

Library of Congress Control Number: 2024948458

Publisher's Cataloging-in-Publication Data

Names: Beattie, Charlie, author.
Title: New York Jets / by Charlie Beattie
Description: Minneapolis, Minnesota: Abdo Publishing, 2026 | Series: Inside the NFL | Includes online resources and index.
Identifiers: ISBN 9781098296865 (lib. bdg.) | ISBN 9798384919384 (ebook)
Subjects: LCSH: New York Jets (Football team)--Juvenile literature. | National Football League--Juvenile literature. | Football teams--Juvenile literature. | American football--Juvenile literature.
Classification: DDC 796.333--dc23

CONTENTS

Jets cornerback Ahmad "Sauce" Gardner lines up against a receiver during a game against the Seattle Seahawks in January 2023.

CHAPTER 1

ROOKIES TAKE FLIGHT

COMING OFF A 4–13 RECORD IN 2021, THE NEW YORK JETS NEEDED help. The good news was that the team entered the next year's National Football League (NFL) Draft with a pair of top-10 picks. Now the team just needed to pick the right two players.

A huge crowd showed up for the draft's first round that April in Las Vegas. The Jets snagged cornerback Ahmad "Sauce" Gardner with the fourth pick. Six picks later, they brought in wide receiver Garrett Wilson. The team hoped Gardner, a college star at Cincinnati, could use his 6-foot-3 frame to shut down opposing receivers. And in former Ohio State standout Wilson, the Jets envisioned a receiver who could burn opposing defenses with his athleticism. All that remained was the rookies proving their skills on the field.

Sauce Gardner, *left*, and Garrett Wilson were first-round draft picks in 2022.

A DYNAMITE DRAFT

The Jets snared two other excellent young players in the 2022 NFL Draft. The team used the 26th pick on linebacker Jermaine Johnson II. In his second season, Johnson picked up 7 1/2 sacks and made the Pro Bowl. In the second round of the 2022 draft, the Jets took promising running back Breece Hall. He rushed for 994 yards and five touchdowns in 2023.

Breece Hall

WILSON WINS IT

After a solid debut in the 2022 season opener, Wilson truly impressed fans in Week 2 against the Cleveland Browns. The Jets trailed the Browns 7–0 early in the second quarter. New York's veteran quarterback Joe Flacco drove the team down to the Browns' 2-yard line. On third down, Wilson lined up on the right side of the field. At the snap of the ball, he stutter-stepped, causing his defender to break toward the middle of the field. Wilson then drifted toward the back corner of the end zone and easily hauled in the pass for his first career touchdown.

Wilson looks for open space after catching a pass against the Cleveland Browns in 2022.

Wilson's breakout performance kept the game close. With 25 seconds left, New York trailed 30–24. Facing third-and-10 from the Browns' 15, Wilson took off up the field. Sensing a soft spot in Cleveland's zone coverage, he then broke to the middle. Flacco hit Wilson in stride, and the rookie ran over the goal line for the tying touchdown. After the extra point, the Jets escaped Cleveland with a 31–30 victory.

Wilson celebrates his game-winning touchdown against the Browns.

SAUCE SEALS IT

Gardner was off to a solid start after the first eight games. He had knocked away 12 passes and grabbed an interception. In Week 9 play against

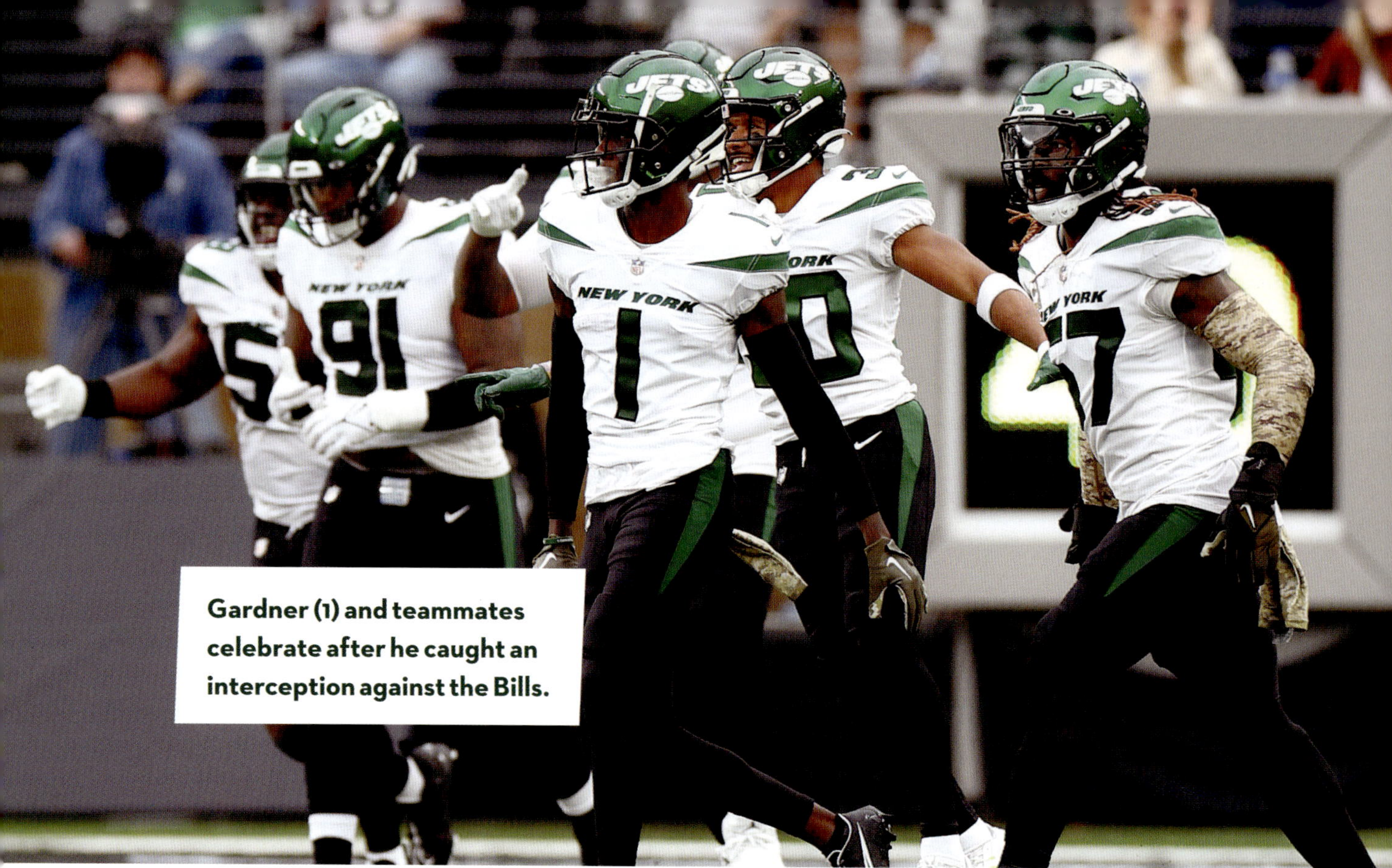

Gardner (1) and teammates celebrate after he caught an interception against the Bills.

the Buffalo Bills, Gardner would show even more skills. As New York trailed 14–10 at the half, the Jets needed a big play.

Gardner tiptoed into position, keeping an eye on the Bills' star quarterback, Josh Allen. As Allen took the snap, Gardner jostled with Bills receiver Gabe Davis at the line of scrimmage. The cornerback then peeled away from Davis just as Allen released the ball. Gardner dropped into the passing lane and plucked the ball out of the air before racing 16 yards to the Buffalo 19. The perfectly timed interception set up New York's go-ahead touchdown.

The Jets held a 20–17 edge in the final seconds. On a last-ditch fourth-down play, Allen heaved the ball deep down the left sideline for Davis. Gardner stayed alongside the wide receiver. At the last second, Gardner knocked the ball away. His big play sealed the win for the Jets.

Gardner knocks the ball away from Buffalo's Gabe Davis on the Bills' final offensive play of the game.

Wilson gives a speech after collecting the Offensive Rookie of the Year Award in February 2023.

AWARD WINNERS

At the end of the season, the NFL handed out its Offensive and Defensive Rookie of the Year Awards. Wilson took home the offensive award after setting Jets rookie records of 83 receptions and 1,103 receiving yards. He also added four touchdowns. Gardner was the defensive award winner. He broke up a league-best 20 passes and intercepted two.

The NFL first presented both awards in 1967. Since then, Gardner and Wilson are just the third set of teammates to win them in the same season. Though the Jets missed the playoffs, their passionate fans knew that with more young talent on the way, their team could be contending for even bigger prizes in the future.

NFL TEAMS MAP

NFC

NFC EAST

DALLAS COWBOYS

NEW YORK GIANTS

PHILADELPHIA EAGLES

WASHINGTON COMMANDERS

NFC WEST

ARIZONA CARDINALS

LOS ANGELES RAMS

SAN FRANCISCO 49ERS

SEATTLE SEAHAWKS

NFC NORTH

CHICAGO BEARS

DETROIT LIONS

GREEN BAY PACKERS

MINNESOTA VIKINGS

NFC SOUTH

ATLANTA FALCONS

CAROLINA PANTHERS

NEW ORLEANS SAINTS

TAMPA BAY BUCCANEERS

AFC

AFC EAST

- BUFFALO BILLS
- MIAMI DOLPHINS
- NEW ENGLAND PATRIOTS
- NEW YORK JETS

AFC WEST

- DENVER BRONCOS
- KANSAS CITY CHIEFS
- LAS VEGAS RAIDERS
- LOS ANGELES CHARGERS

AFC NORTH

- BALTIMORE RAVENS
- CINCINNATI BENGALS
- CLEVELAND BROWNS
- PITTSBURGH STEELERS

AFC SOUTH

- HOUSTON TEXANS
- INDIANAPOLIS COLTS
- JACKSONVILLE JAGUARS
- TENNESSEE TITANS

New York Titans staff members, including team owner Harry Wismer, *front center*, pose for a photo in 1960.

CHAPTER 2

REMEMBER THE TITANS

IN THE LATE 1950S, WITH THE POPULARITY OF FOOTBALL BOOMING, eight potential team owners got together to form a new professional league. They wanted to compete with the NFL for fans. That's how the American Football League (AFL) was born.

The new league placed most of its teams in cities that did not have NFL teams. But the owners knew that if the AFL was going to survive, it needed a team in New York City. The Big Apple was not only the country's largest urban area but also a media hub. Placing a team there would show that the league was serious.

Harry Wismer stepped up to become the owner of the New York AFL franchise. Wismer had been a popular radio and television announcer. He was a natural showman who knew that getting AFL games on television was one

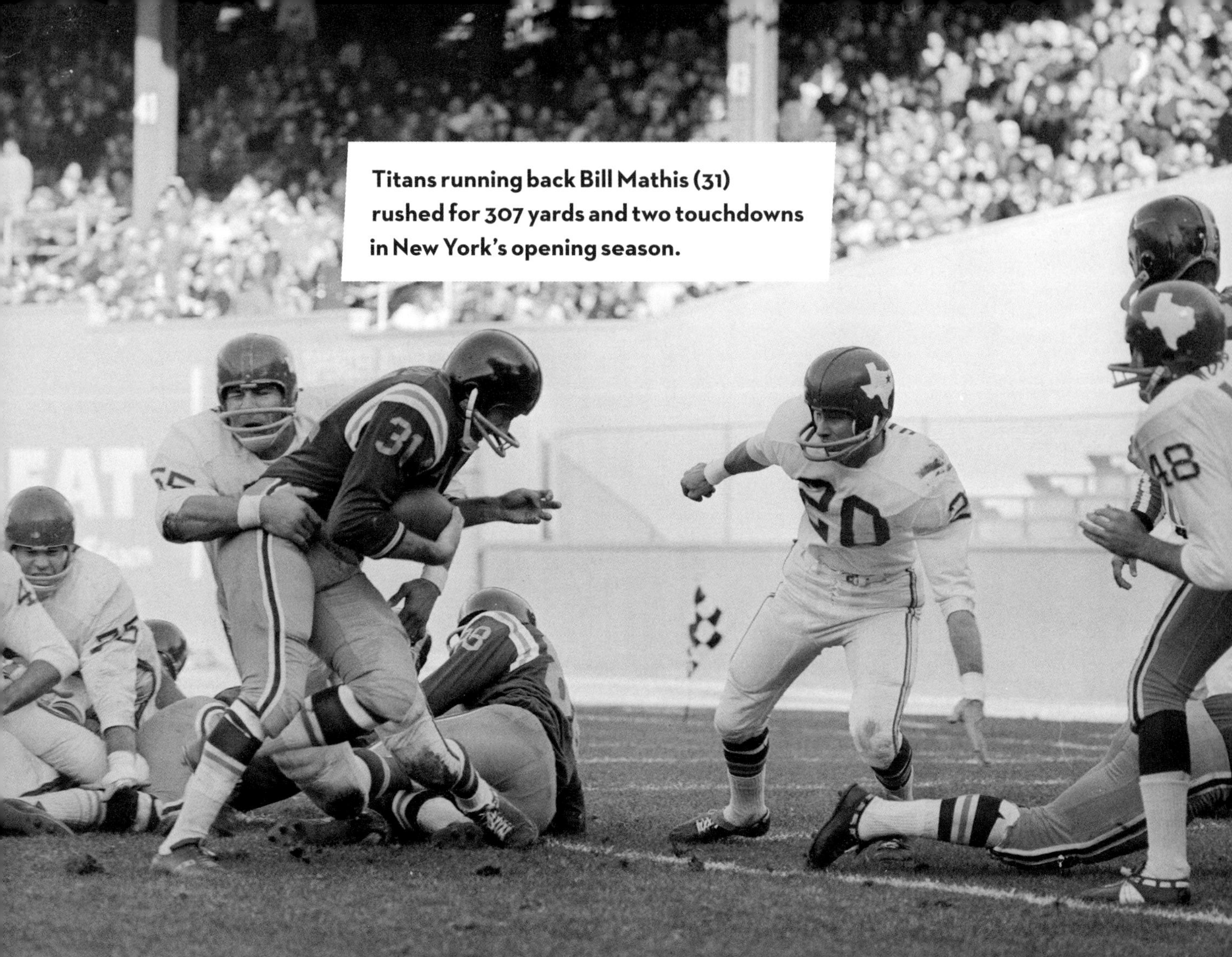
Titans running back Bill Mathis (31) rushed for 307 yards and two touchdowns in New York's opening season.

way the league could thrive. He helped negotiate a deal with the ABC television network to televise AFL games each week.

Wismer believed the team would need to outdo the NFL's popular and successful New York Giants right away. With that in mind, Wismer named his new team the Titans. When asked why, he said, "Because titans are bigger and stronger than giants."

"TITANS ARE BIGGER AND STRONGER THAN GIANTS."

—HARRY WISMER

A ROUGH START

Wismer had big plans for his team, but he didn't have much money. The Titans' early players got little pay—if they got paid at all. In the team's first few seasons, players were so worried about collecting their checks that many chose not to shower after practices. That way they could race over to the one bank that could cash their paychecks before their teammates. The bank had only so much cash available to give out. Anyone who got there after the bank ran out of funds didn't get their money that week.

Player paychecks weren't the only shabby thing about the Titans. The team played at the Polo Grounds. Though situated in a central spot on the island of Manhattan, the stadium had not been used in three years when the Titans started playing there. It was run down and dirty. And with the Titans struggling on the field, few fans wanted to visit the dingy building. AFL commissioner Joe Foss

New York's iconic Polo Grounds stadium stood from 1911 until 1964.

stated that during one visit to see the team play, he walked through the stands and shook hands with every fan who showed up.

The Titans were coached by Sammy Baugh, who had been one of the NFL's all-time best quarterbacks. But Baugh wasn't as successful as a coach. Though he led the team to a pair of 7–7 seasons in 1960 and 1961, he was deeply unhappy. A laid-back Texan, Baugh hated both the busy pace of New York and the dirty Polo Grounds. Wismer took steps to put the team in a better facility, signing an agreement to play in the planned Shea Stadium. The new stadium, located in the borough of Queens, was scheduled to open in 1962. But construction problems delayed the opening two years.

Coach Sammy Baugh had played for Washington from 1937 to 1952.

After the struggles of the first two seasons, Wismer wanted to fire Baugh, but he had one problem. Baugh had a year left on his contract, and if he were fired, Wismer would owe the coach $20,000. Wismer was quickly going bankrupt and didn't have that kind of money. Instead, Wismer simply didn't tell Baugh where the Titans were holding training camp before the 1962 season. Baugh figured it out anyway and showed up, but he saw that Clyde "Bulldog" Turner was now the head coach. Baugh simply stuck it out for the season as an assistant and collected his paychecks.

BIG CHANGES

The Titans' 5–9 record in 1962 was just the start of their problems. They were still drawing few fans and running out of money. Rather than let the team fail, the other AFL owners took over the Titans. A year later, they sold the team to Sonny Werblin.

Sonny Werblin shows off the Jets' new helmet design after buying the team in 1963.

The new owner made huge changes. The Titans had played in navy blue and gold uniforms. Werblin changed the team colors to kelly green and white. The team would finally start playing at Shea Stadium. Shea sat right between New York's two major airports.

TV DEALS

Harry Wismer negotiated the AFL's first TV deal with ABC in 1960. It paid each team about $100,000 per year. At the time, other networks were paying NFL teams around $950,000 each. When Sonny Werblin bought the Jets, he renegotiated the deal so that AFL teams made nearly the same amount as NFL teams. The raise helped AFL teams compete for top players, and it eventually helped force a merger between the two leagues.

Inspired by the planes that were constantly flying overhead, Werblin renamed the football team the Jets.

Werblin's last big change was a new head coach. He hired Weeb Ewbank, who had just been let go by the NFL's Baltimore Colts. Ewbank had led the Colts for nearly a decade, and he had won two NFL titles. His new job was to turn the Jets around.

FLYING HIGH

For their first game of the 1964 season, the Jets hosted the Denver Broncos. More than 45,000 fans showed up at Shea Stadium to watch New York win 30–6. It was the first of many big crowds for a team that was suddenly a hot New York ticket. On November 8, more than 60,000 turned up as New York took on the Buffalo Bills. The Jets lost 20–7 against a Buffalo team that was on its way to a league championship, but the game was still a

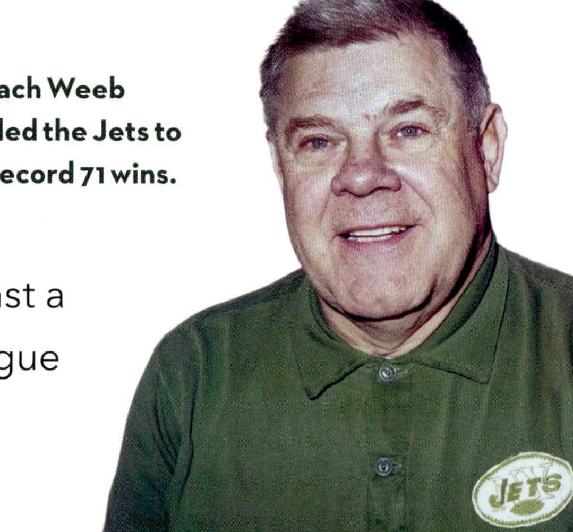

Head coach Weeb Ewbank led the Jets to a team-record 71 wins.

Moving to Shea Stadium in 1964 helped make the Jets a major player in the New York sports landscape.

milestone for New York and the AFL. It was the first time more than 60,000 fans attended any AFL game.

New York won only five games for the third straight season in 1964, but the team was quietly improving. Before the season, the Jets had scored a huge victory over their NFL rivals, the Giants. Both teams had selected talented fullback Matt Snell in their league's draft. They then started a bidding war over the young star. In the end, Snell signed with the Jets, who promised him a starting role.

Wide receiver Don Maynard caught at least eight touchdown passes in seven seasons with the Jets.

A bulldozing runner, Snell finished the season second in the league with 948 rushing yards. He also caught 56 passes.

The Jets had other budding stars in the 1964 season. Speedy receiver Don Maynard caught eight touchdown passes. On defense, safety Dainard Paulson led the AFL with 12 interceptions. Rugged linebacker Larry Grantham, who had been with the team since its first season, emerged as a team leader.

BROADWAY JOE

While the Jets gained talent in 1964, they reached a new level in 1965 with the addition of rookie quarterback Joe Namath. The star passer had just finished a stellar season at Alabama. The Jets drafted him and then made a huge splash by paying him $427,000 for a three-year contract. This was the largest contract in the history of football at the time.

In Namath, the Jets had a true star. He was charismatic and good looking. The young quarterback lived a flashy lifestyle in New York.

Quarterback Joe Namath, *right*, signs his first contract with the Jets as coach Weeb Ewbank, *left*, and owner Sonny Werblin look on.

His teammates, however, didn't initially know what to make of their new quarterback. Namath made far more money than they did, and many Jets resented giving such a high salary to a rookie. In 1965, Namath appeared on the cover of *Sports Illustrated* magazine under the headline "Football Goes Show Biz." The photo featured Namath standing in front of the marquee lights of the city's famous Broadway district. After seeing the photo, Jets tackle Sherman Plunkett started calling Namath "Broadway Joe." The nickname stuck.

Underneath Namath's huge celebrity, however, the quarterback was a tough football player.

Lineman Sherman Plunkett played for the Jets from 1963 to 1967.

Maynard led the team with more than 1,200 receiving yards in 1965.

He entered the AFL with a bad knee from a college injury at Alabama. It wasn't long before he was playing on two injured knees. But Namath fought through the pain, zipping passes right on target to Maynard and George Sauer. When his teammates saw Namath get up after every hit to keep driving the team forward, they changed their minds about their celebrity quarterback.

It helped that Namath had turned the Jets into a strong team. In 1967, New York had its first winning season, finishing 8–5–1 and narrowly missing the AFL Championship Game. Namath threw for 4,007 yards. No quarterback in the history of football had ever thrown for more. New York was finally a contender, but an even better season was yet to come.

Namath led the AFL in passing yards in both 1966 and 1967.

Jets guard Bob Talamini, *left*, talks with center John Schmitt during a game in 1968.

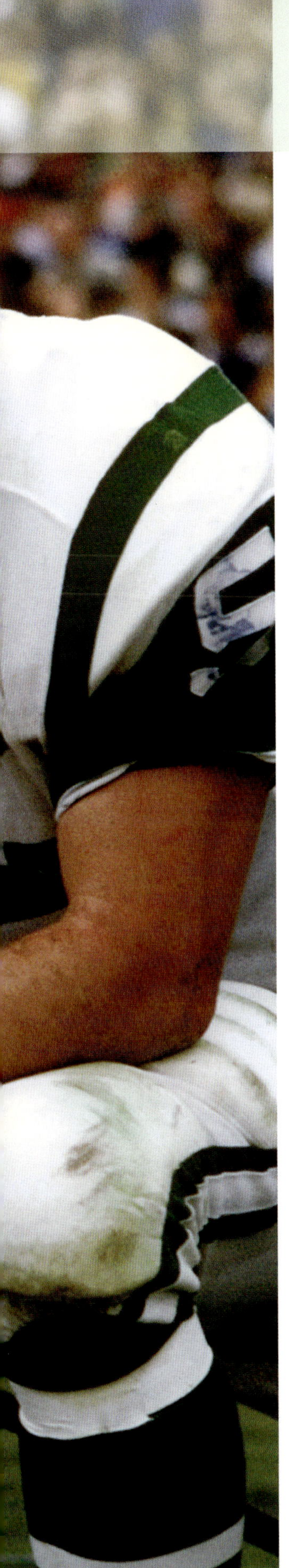

CHAPTER 3

WE'RE GOING TO WIN THE GAME

WHEN THE AFL STARTED, FEW EXPECTED IT TO SUCCEED. INSTEAD, THE AFL proved so popular that the NFL agreed in 1966 to merge with the upstart league. The AFL teams were set to join the older league in 1970. But starting in 1966, their champions began meeting in an ultimate title game, which is now known as the Super Bowl. The NFL's Green Bay Packers thumped the AFL's Kansas City Chiefs 35–10 in Super Bowl I. The next year, the Packers routed the Oakland Raiders 33–14.

To NFL fans, the lopsided results proved what they already believed: the NFL was much better than the AFL. The only people who seemed to think otherwise were AFL players, coaches, and owners. But they had to prove it on the field.

Coming into the 1968 season, the Jets knew they had a great chance to represent the AFL in

Super Bowl III. But the year didn't start well. After five games, the Jets were just 3-2. And their losses had come against the lowly Buffalo Bills and Denver Broncos.

After beating the Houston Oilers 20-14 in Week 6, the Jets' offense began to click. New York scored at least 25 points in each of the final eight games of the season. The Jets won seven of them to finish the season 11-3 and easily win the AFL's East Division.

THE HEIDI GAME

On November 17, 1968, the Jets led the Oakland Raiders 32-29 with 1:05 left. NBC was showing the game on television across the country but cut away at 7:00 p.m. to show the children's movie *Heidi*. That caused football fans to miss a thrilling finish, as the Raiders scored twice in nine seconds and won 43-32. Furious fans complained to NBC, and the game changed how football broadcasts were handled. After that, games were shown until they were over, even if they overlapped other shows.

A LONG ONE

That set up a playoff showdown with the West Division champions, the Raiders, who had beaten the Jets during the regular season. Despite playing on opposite sides of the country, the two teams had developed a strong rivalry. But since Joe Namath's arrival in New York in 1965, the Jets had beaten Oakland only once.

Playing at Shea Stadium, the Jets jumped out to an early lead. Namath threw a touchdown pass to Don Maynard, then Jim Turner kicked a field goal to put New York up 10–0. But the Raiders battled back. In the fourth quarter, Oakland went up 23–20.

Namath and Maynard knew they could get the lead back. Maynard told his quarterback, "I've got a long one when you need it." On the second play of the drive, Namath heaved a bomb down the right sideline for his speedy receiver. The wind blew the ball over Maynard's head, but he twisted his body to make the catch before falling at the Oakland 6-yard line.

Receiver George Sauer led the Jets with 66 receptions in 1968.

The pair connected again on the next play, with Namath scrambling before throwing a low pass to Maynard in the end zone with 7:47 left in the game. After this touchdown, the Jets' stout defense managed to stop Oakland three times in the game's final seven minutes to preserve the 27–23 win. The Jets were on their way to the Super Bowl in Miami.

Jim Turner (11) kicks one of his two field goals against the Oakland Raiders in the AFL title game in December 1968.

THE GUARANTEE

The Jets entered Super Bowl III as huge underdogs to the NFL-champion Baltimore Colts. And in the two weeks leading up to the game, members of the national media said that while the Jets were a nice story, they were about to be crushed by the latest great NFL team. After all, the 13–1 Colts had allowed only 10.3 points per game, the lowest average in more than two decades.

After studying the Baltimore Colts' strengths and weaknesses on defense, quarterback Joe Namath and the Jets were sure they could win Super Bowl III.

While studying Baltimore's defense on film, the Jets realized that the Colts overwhelmed offenses with a heavy blitz. As soon as the Jets figured that out, their confidence grew. They knew that one of Namath's strengths was reading blitzes and getting passes off quickly before the pass rushers could hit him.

By the Thursday before the game, the Jets were quietly confident they could win. Namath was attending a banquet at the Miami Touchdown Club that night, where he was given an award. As he got up to speak, a fan in the back of the room shouted that the Colts were going to dominate the game. By that point, Namath was fed up. He shot back, "Hey, buddy. I've got news for you. We're going to win the game. I guarantee it."

"I'VE GOT NEWS FOR YOU. WE'RE GOING TO WIN THE GAME. I GUARANTEE IT."

—JOE NAMATH ON SUPER BOWL III

When Weeb Ewbank heard of Namath's boast, the Jets' head coach was furious. In the locker room with the team the next day, Ewbank confronted his quarterback in front of the rest of the team. Namath coolly responded, "Don't you think we're gonna win, Coach?"

MAKING HISTORY

Both the Jets and Colts struggled on offense through a scoreless first quarter. It was the New York defense that made the first big play of the game. Early in the second, Baltimore faced third-and-4 at the Jets' 6-yard line. Colts quarterback Earl Morrall went back to pass. But the ball bounced off the intended receiver's shoulder pads, and Jets defensive back Randy Beverly made a tumbling interception in the end zone.

Namath and the offense then moved like a machine down the field. Namath completed four passes, and running backs Matt Snell and Emerson Boozer did the rest. Snell gained 35 yards on the ground during the drive and another 12 through the air. He capped the march with a 4-yard touchdown run off the left side, barreling past two Colts defenders at the goal line.

It was New York's only touchdown of the game, but it didn't matter. The Jets defense frustrated Morrall, who had been the NFL's Most Valuable Player (MVP) that season. Late in the second quarter, Morrall drove the Colts to the Jets' 15-yard line, but New York's Johnny Sample intercepted the next pass. The Colts got the ball back in New York territory with 43 seconds left until halftime. Two plays later, Jets cornerback Jim Hudson picked off a pass to preserve New York's 7–0 lead.

Jets running back Matt Snell rushed for 121 yards on 30 carries and had four receptions for 40 yards in Super Bowl III.

Namath kept New York moving in the third quarter. He barely called any plays in the huddle. Instead, he would walk to the line of scrimmage and see how the Colts were lined up. From there, he would make a call to beat whatever defensive tactic Baltimore had planned. His ability to beat the Colts' blitzes kept him one step ahead of the favored NFL team. In the second half, Namath guided the Jets to three scoring drives that all ended in field goals by Turner. With 14 minutes to go, the Jets led 16–0.

By now, Baltimore had turned to Johnny Unitas at quarterback. Unitas had been a superstar earlier in his career. Some considered him the best to ever play the position. However, he was 35 years old and had missed nearly the entire season with an injury. Like Morrall, Unitas was able to move the Colts deep into New York territory. But on second-and-10 from the Jets' 25, Unitas underthrew a pass to receiver Jimmy Orr at the goal line. Beverly cut in front of the receiver for his second pick of the day.

Cornerback Jim Hudson returns the ball after an interception in Super Bowl III.

The Colts scored a touchdown late in the game, but the Jets walked away with a hard-fought 16–7 victory. It was one of the most shocking upsets in sports history. The Jets proved that the AFL was indeed good enough to square off with NFL teams.

Though Namath didn't have a great statistical game, his stellar play calling helped him earn MVP honors in Super Bowl III.

Namath's guarantee is still seen as one of football's most iconic moments, helping the Super Bowl become a must-see event. And after the game, he created another memorable image. He jogged off the field with his index finger held in the air, signifying that the Jets were the sport's number one team.

Jets linebacker Gerry Philbin hits Colts quarterback Johnny Unitas in the fourth quarter of Super Bowl III.

GROUNDED

Namath guided the Jets to another AFL East championship in 1969, but New York didn't make it past its first playoff game. From there, the team started to go downhill. New York joined the NFL in 1970, along with the rest of the AFL teams. The Jets then didn't put a winning team on the field for the next decade.

One of the biggest reasons for this was Namath's health. When he played, the Jets were capable of magic. However, as the years wore on, the star quarterback's bad knees only got worse. Between 1970 and 1976, Namath appeared in all 14 games of a

Jets players congratulate coach Weeb Ewbank after the team's 16–7 win over the Colts in Super Bowl III.

season only twice. After a 1976 season in which he threw just four touchdown passes against 16 interceptions, the 33-year-old was cut. The move marked the end of the Jets' incredible Super Bowl story. And it would be a long time before the team created another happy memory for its passionate fans.

Walt Michaels served as an assistant coach with the Jets before becoming the team's head coach in 1977.

FLYING LOW

In 1977, the Jets promoted Walt Michaels to head coach. Michaels had been a longtime Jets assistant coach. The fiery, opinionated former linebacker brought a snarl to the sideline.

Michaels didn't win much right away. In his first season, the Jets finished just 3–11. But slowly the team started putting together a strong roster. Many of the players signed by Michaels and president Jim Kensil became fan favorites.

In 1977, the team took speedy receiver Wesley Walker in the second round of the draft. He played 13 years for the Jets, racking up more receiving yards than any team receiver except Don Maynard. Later in that same draft, the Jets selected defensive lineman Joe Klecko. Known for his high-energy style of play, Klecko was one of the most versatile linemen in NFL history.

In his career, he was named to the Pro Bowl as a defensive end, defensive tackle, and nose tackle, something no other NFL player had done.

The Jets continued adding key players over the next few years. New York picked up tight end Mickey Shuler in the 1978 draft. In 1979, New York added flashy pass rusher Mark Gastineau and skilled run stopper Marty Lyons.

Jets wide receiver Wesley Walker leaps to haul in a pass against the San Francisco 49ers in 1986.

THE NEW YORK SACK EXCHANGE

The Jets' new talent finally came together to produce a good team in 1981. After starting the season 1–3–1, the Jets won nine of their final 11 games to reach the playoffs for the first time since the 1969 season. A big reason why was the play of Gastineau, Klecko, Lyons, and veteran Abdul Salaam along the defensive line. Sacks didn't become an official statistic until the next season, but the

Defensive lineman Joe Klecko was named to the Pro Bowl four times in 11 seasons with the Jets.

foursome took down quarterbacks 54 times in 1981. Along the way, they picked up the nickname "the New York Sack Exchange."

The team's quarterback was Richard Todd, who had been a first-round draft pick in 1976. Like Joe Namath before him, Todd had played for Alabama. That connection meant he was always compared to the team's legendary star. For his first few seasons, Todd struggled to live up to Namath. But in 1981, he finally broke out with 25 touchdown passes. Fans at Shea Stadium began bringing "In Todd We Trust" banners to games. But even Todd's magical season couldn't save the Jets in that year's playoffs. The team fell behind the Buffalo Bills 24–0 in the first half. New York rallied, scoring three touchdowns. But the Jets came up short in a season-ending 31–27 loss.

Quarterback Richard Todd threw 110 touchdown passes in eight years with the Jets.

THE MUD BOWL

New York running back Freeman McNeil averaged more than 5 yards per carry during his stellar 1982 season.

The Jets selected running back Freeman McNeil with the third pick in the 1981 draft. One year later, McNeil led the NFL in rushing. The season was interrupted by a players' strike after Week 2, but in nine games, the lightning-fast McNeil racked up 786 yards and six touchdowns as the Jets finished 6–3 to reach the playoffs again. McNeil then piled up 202 yards and a touchdown and also threw a touchdown pass in New York's 44–17 romp over the Cincinnati Bengals in the wild-card round. After beating the Los Angeles Raiders 17–14, the Jets were set to face the division-rival Miami Dolphins in the conference title game.

Miami had beaten the Jets twice during the regular season, but New York felt it had the faster team. However, it rained for three days leading up to the game in Miami. The Dolphins didn't cover the field, and it turned into a soggy mess. Michaels was furious, thinking

Miami linebacker A. J. Duhe, *right*, intercepts a pass from Todd in the fourth quarter of "the Mud Bowl" in January 1983.

that Miami coach Don Shula left the field uncovered intentionally to slow down the Jets. Shula responded by saying the Dolphins didn't even own a tarp.

With the slop limiting their ground attack, the Jets lost the game known as "the Mud Bowl" 14–0. Todd threw five interceptions. Three of them went to linebacker A. J. Duhe, whose 35-yard touchdown return in the fourth quarter sealed New York's fate. Later, Klecko said, "If anyone asks me about the most disappointing time in your life as a football player, that is the most disappointing."

"IF ANYONE ASKS ME ABOUT THE MOST DISAPPOINTING TIME IN YOUR LIFE AS A FOOTBALL PLAYER, THAT IS THE MOST DISAPPOINTING."

—JOE KLECKO ON THE MUD BOWL

NEW JERSEY BOUND

Michaels resigned after the playoff loss to Miami. Under new coach Joe Walton, the team stumbled to 7-9 the next year as Todd threw 26 interceptions. It took New York another two years to reach the postseason again. The biggest Jets news in that time came from off the field. In 1984, the team moved out of Shea Stadium and into Giants Stadium. Fans were upset to share a field with their city rivals, and they also disliked that Giants Stadium was not in New York. It was located across the river in East Rutherford, New Jersey. Since that day, neither New York team has actually played in the city for which it is named.

Jets fans tear down the goalpost in the team's last game at Shea Stadium before moving to New Jersey.

The new home didn't end the Jets' string of playoff disappointments. The team finished 11-5 in 1985 but lost in the wild-card round to the New England Patriots. A year later, after a 10-6 finish, the Jets beat the Kansas City Chiefs 35-15 in the wild-card round. They were powered by a 135-yard rushing performance from McNeil. The next week, New York traveled to

Cleveland to face the Browns. The Jets led 20–10 after a touchdown run by McNeil late in the fourth quarter. But then the team unraveled.

The biggest mistake came from one of the Jets' most popular stars. Gastineau was a dominant pass rusher. In 1984, he had 22 sacks, setting an NFL record that stood until 2001. He punctuated them with his signature "sack dance," which both angered opponents and energized New York's supporters. Future Hall of Famer Michael Strahan, who would later break Gastineau's record, said, "Mark made the defensive end position a glamorous position. You didn't get a sack and go back to the huddle. You got up and did that Gastineau dance, the sack dance, the crazy man dance." It wouldn't be long before many other NFL defenders created their own signature moves to celebrate big plays.

Defensive end Mark Gastineau celebrates a sack.

However, against the Browns, Gastineau's relentless pursuit of the quarterback cost the Jets. On the next drive after McNeil's touchdown, Gastineau was called for roughing the passer on a second-and-24 play for Cleveland. The 15-yard penalty gave the Browns new life. Cleveland scored 10 points to tie the game. The Browns went on to beat the Jets in double overtime.

Defensive lineman Marty Lyons pumps his fist after making a tackle.

Bill Parcells also served as the Jets' general manager during the late 1990s.

AN UGLY STRETCH

Though Jets fans were disappointed in the team's playoff failures, it was better than missing the postseason completely. But that's what New York did for the rest of the 1980s and most of the early 1990s. An 8–8 finish and a wild-card loss in 1991 was the best the team did over a 10-year stretch. The Jets bottomed out in 1996 by finishing 1–15 under coach Rich Kotite.

After that season, New York made a bold move. The Jets traded several draft picks to the New England Patriots for head coach Bill Parcells. A stern disciplinarian and master motivator, Parcells had just taken New England to the Super Bowl. He also won a pair of championships with the Giants after the 1986 and 1990 seasons.

Within two years, Parcells had turned the Jets around. In 1998, veteran quarterback Vinny Testaverde linked up with former top draft pick Keyshawn Johnson and undrafted fan favorite Wayne Chrebet in the passing game. Running back Curtis Martin, also signed from the Patriots, rushed for nearly 1,300 yards. New York

PARCELLS TO THE JETS

Bill Parcells's contract with the New England Patriots prevented him from becoming the Jets' head coach. So New York tried a clever work-around. The Jets hired New England's defensive coordinator, Bill Belichick, as head coach, while Parcells came aboard as a consultant. When the Patriots complained about the sneaky move, the NFL stepped in and worked out a trade. The Jets sent four draft picks to New England. In return, Parcells came to the Jets as head coach and Belichick became New York's defensive coordinator.

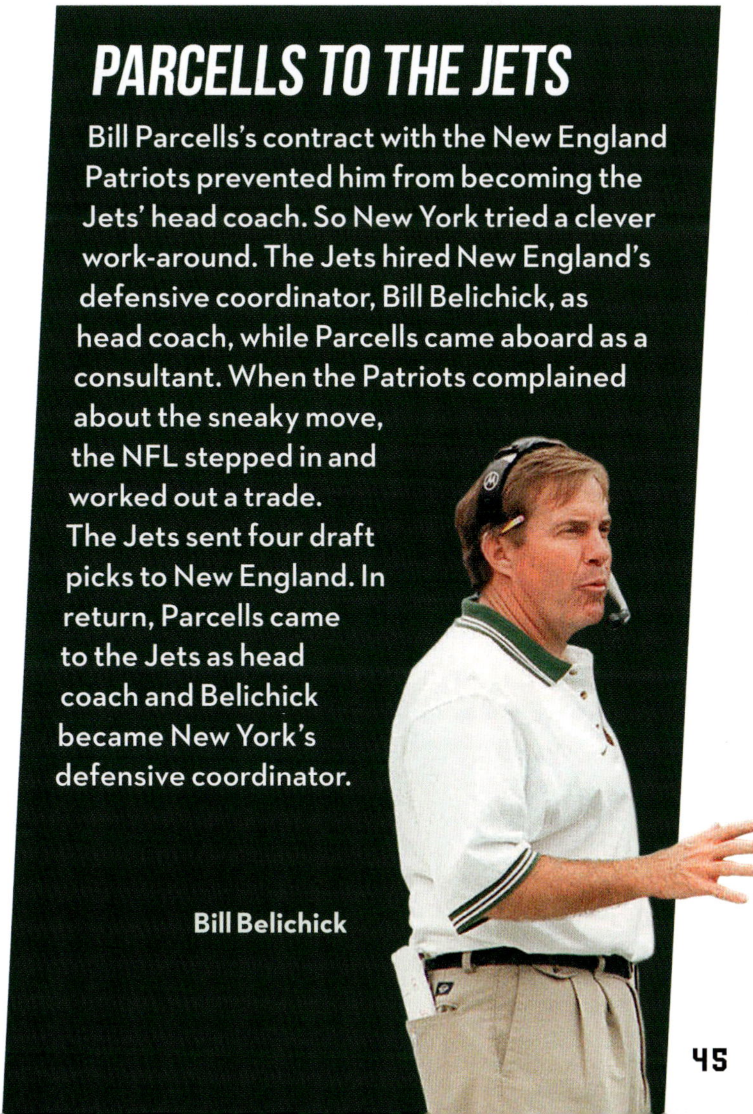

Bill Belichick

Wide receiver Wayne Chrebet joined the Jets in 1995 after playing at nearby Hofstra University. He had 580 catches in 11 seasons with the team.

finished a franchise-best 12–4 and captured its first division title since the 1970 merger.

The Jets looked like a true Super Bowl contender after dispatching the Jacksonville Jaguars 34–24 in the divisional round. But as with previous playoff appearances, New York came undone with one bad performance. Testaverde had thrown only seven interceptions all season, but in the conference title game, he was picked off twice by the Denver Broncos. The Jets threw away a 10–0 lead and lost 23–10, once again coming up a step short of the Super Bowl. Parcells spent one more year with the Jets before retiring.

Jets quarterback Vinny Testaverde was named to the Pro Bowl in 1998 after throwing for 3,256 yards and 29 touchdowns.

Bill Belichick talks to the media after resigning from the Jets' head coaching job in January 2000.

PREPARING FOR TAKEOFF

In early January 2000, the Jets announced Bill Belichick as the team's new head coach. One day later, Belichick called another press conference. In it, he said he had changed his mind.

Within a month, Belichick was the head coach of the New England Patriots. There, he built a dynasty. The other American Football Conference (AFC) East teams spent the next several years chasing Belichick's Patriots.

The Jets started that chase with Al Groh as head coach. The 2000 season began well, and New York took a 5–1 record into a matchup with the Miami Dolphins on *Monday Night Football*. After three quarters, the stunned Jets trailed 30–7. But quarterback Vinny Testaverde led a stirring comeback with four touchdown passes in the final 15 minutes. His fourth, with 42 seconds

Jets offensive tackle Jumbo Elliott bobbles the ball before holding on to his key touchdown during "the Monday Night Miracle" in 2000.

left, was a lob pass to offensive tackle John "Jumbo" Elliott, who had lined up at tight end on the play. The 6-foot-7-inch Elliott juggled the ball while making a diving catch in the end zone to tie the game 37–37. The Jets won on a field goal in overtime.

"The Monday Night Miracle" was the high point of the Jets' season. The team won only three games the rest of the way. After the meltdown left the 9–7 Jets outside the playoffs, Groh resigned and took a job coaching college football.

PLAYING TO WIN

In Groh's place, the Jets hired former NFL defensive back Herman Edwards. Edwards was an intense competitor and a passionate coach. That was especially clear after a 24–21 loss to the Cleveland Browns on October 27, 2002. The Jets fell to 2–5 after the defeat, and a few days later, a reporter asked if Edwards was worried about the team quitting on the season. Edwards was furious. Staring directly at the reporter who asked the question, he erupted. "You play to win the game!" Edwards shouted. "Hello? You play to win the game. You don't just play to play it."

"YOU PLAY TO WIN THE GAME!"

—HERMAN EDWARDS

The speech became an instant sensation. The quote defined Edwards's NFL coaching career. It also fired up his team. New York responded by finishing the season at 9-7 to win the AFC East title. New York then pummeled the Indianapolis Colts 41-0 in the wild-card round before falling in the divisional round to the Oakland Raiders.

The Jets douse coach Herman Edwards with Gatorade after winning the AFC East title in 2002.

The Jets had plenty of talent in the early 2000s. Curtis Martin remained one of the top running backs in the NFL. Quarterback Chad Pennington didn't have the biggest arm, but he was a precise passer who connected well with receivers Wayne Chrebet,

Laveranues Coles, and Santana Moss. Meanwhile, the stout linebacking corps of Sam Cowart, Marvin Jones, and Mo Lewis led the defense.

Even with that talent, the Jets were looking up at the dominant Patriots. Belichick had won three Super Bowls in New England by the end of the 2005 season. Back in New York, Edwards was struggling for consistency. He left for a new coaching job in Kansas City after the Jets finished 4–12 in 2005.

The Jets replaced Edwards with Eric Mangini, who had been New England's defensive coordinator. Yet another coach heading from one team to the other fueled the already heated rivalry between the two teams. Mangini fanned those flames even more when he accused the Patriots of illegally taping New York's practices in 2007. The NFL backed up the Jets, fined the Patriots, and stripped New England of a first-round draft pick. Still, Mangini's team struggled on the field. In three seasons, his Jets went just 2–5 against New England.

Curtis Martin retired in 2007 as the Jets' all-time leading rusher with 10,302 yards.

Center Kevin Mawae was named to the Pro Bowl six times while playing for the Jets between 1998 and 2005.

Head coach Rex Ryan celebrates a play during the playoffs in January 2010.

REX AND THE SANCHIZE

Rex Ryan came from a prominent coaching family. His brother Rob was a successful defensive coordinator. Their father, Buddy, had been a Jets assistant in Super Bowl III. Buddy went on to become an iconic defensive coach.

The three Ryans weren't shy about sharing their opinions. So when Rex was hired by the Jets as head coach in 2009, he made it very clear that he was there to take down the Patriots. In a radio interview, Ryan said he hadn't come to New York to "kiss Bill Belichick's [Super Bowl] rings." Many wrote off Ryan as a loudmouth, but he quickly improved the team.

Ryan wasn't the only new face in New York. Jets fans were ecstatic when the team traded up to pick quarterback Mark Sanchez in the 2009 draft. Strong-armed, charismatic, and confident, Sanchez had the look of a future star. Fans immediately dubbed him "the Sanchize," a play on the word *franchise*.

Sanchez didn't shine right away, but he didn't have to. The Jets had a strong defense led by thumping linebacker Bart Scott and safeties Jim Leonhard and Kerry Rhodes. Opposing quarterbacks avoided cornerback Darrelle Revis so much that receivers going against the Jets star were said to be stranded on "Revis Island." New York finished 9–7 during the 2009 regular season but turned it on in the playoffs. Revis intercepted passes in both the wild-card and divisional rounds as the Jets advanced to the AFC title game. There, the defense crumbled in a 30–17 loss to the Indianapolis Colts.

The Jets selected quarterback Mark Sanchez (6) with the fifth pick in the 2009 NFL Draft.

THE SHOWDOWN

In Week 2 of the 2010 season, the Jets thumped New England 28–14. Later that year, New England returned the favor with a 45–3

Though quarterbacks rarely threw his way, Darrelle Revis still recorded 25 interceptions in eight seasons with the Jets.

blowout win. All along, the teams sparred in the media, especially leading up to their third meeting in the divisional playoffs.

The night before the game, Ryan brought in former Jets player Dennis Byrd to speak to his team. Byrd had been a rising star with the Jets when he was paralyzed in a 1992 game. After his passionate speech, the Jets were fired up to take on their rival.

Sanchez had one of his best games in a New York uniform. With the Jets leading 14–11 early in the fourth quarter, he lobbed a pass to receiver Santonio Holmes, who made a diving catch in the corner of the end zone. It was one of three scoring passes on the day for the second-year quarterback, and New York won 28–21.

After the game, Jets fans were thrilled that they had finally taken down the mighty Patriots. But those good feelings didn't last.

Jets receiver Santonio Holmes celebrates after catching a touchdown pass in New York's divisional-round win over the Patriots in January 2011.

Despite several disappointing years, Jets fans remained passionate for the team.

New York fell behind the Pittsburgh Steelers 24–0 in the AFC title game. Despite a spirited comeback, the Jets lost 24–19.

SAME OLD JETS

Though New York seemed on the verge of a breakthrough, the opposite happened. Sanchez never delivered on his early promise. He was eventually let go after the 2012 season. Ryan was fired after the Jets finished 4–12 in 2014. It was the Jets' fourth consecutive season outside the playoffs. The team had made a lot of noise in Ryan's time in charge, but New York still had not been to the Super Bowl since the late 1960s.

Though the team had rarely been successful in the 50 years following its one championship, the passion of Jets fans has never faded. When bad things happen to the team, they often laugh and repeat the phrase "same old Jets." Unfortunately, the team gave them plenty of opportunities to repeat that phrase through the 2010s. As the Jets churned through a series of failed first-round

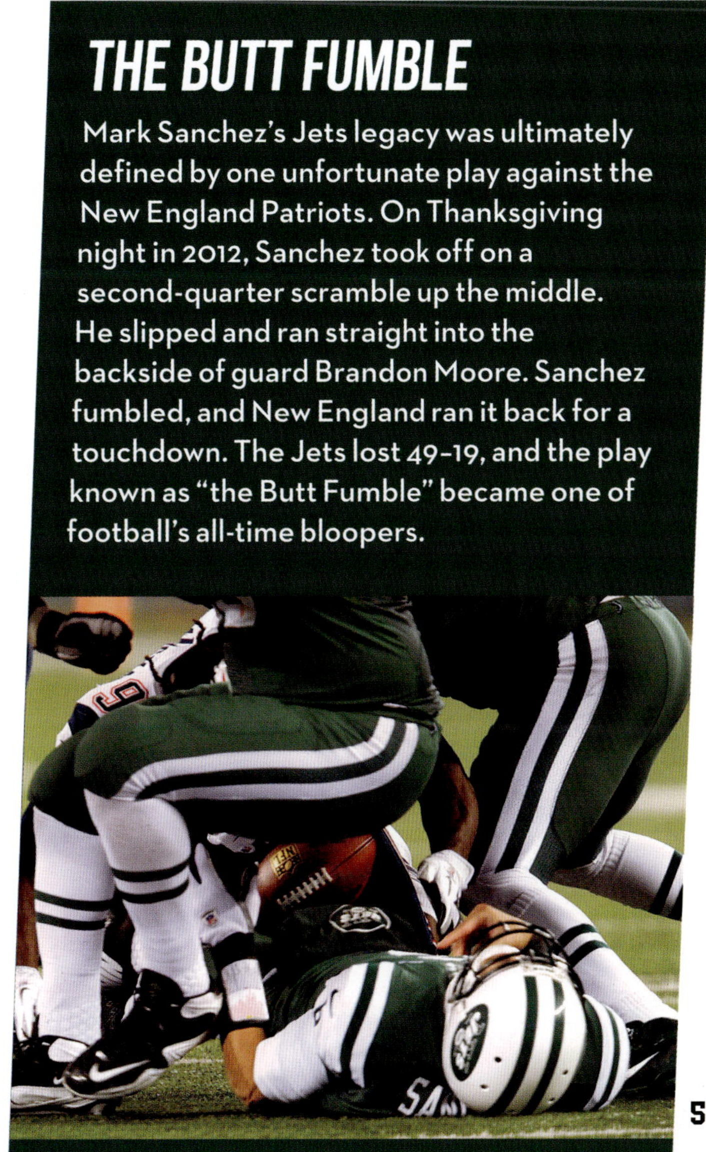

THE BUTT FUMBLE

Mark Sanchez's Jets legacy was ultimately defined by one unfortunate play against the New England Patriots. On Thanksgiving night in 2012, Sanchez took off on a second-quarter scramble up the middle. He slipped and ran straight into the backside of guard Brandon Moore. Sanchez fumbled, and New England ran it back for a touchdown. The Jets lost 49–19, and the play known as "the Butt Fumble" became one of football's all-time bloopers.

JETS TROPHY CASE

SUPER BOWL CHAMPIONSHIPS: 1

Super Bowl III – January 12, 1969

AFL CHAMPIONSHIPS: 1

1968

DIVISION TITLES: 4

AFL East: 1968, 1969
AFC East: 1998, 2002

All stats are through the 2024 season.

quarterbacks, New York finished last in the AFC East six times in seven years from 2016 to 2022.

In 2023, the Jets brought in 39-year-old former MVP quarterback Aaron Rodgers. They hoped Rodgers was the missing piece for a team that featured talented young players such as receiver Garrett Wilson and cornerback Sauce Gardner. But just four plays into his first season, Rodgers tore his left Achilles tendon and was out for the year. Though he returned in 2024, the Jets failed to take flight. Coach Robert Saleh was fired after five frustrating games. It was clear the Jets were still looking for the right combination to rekindle the magic of their long-ago Super Bowl glory.

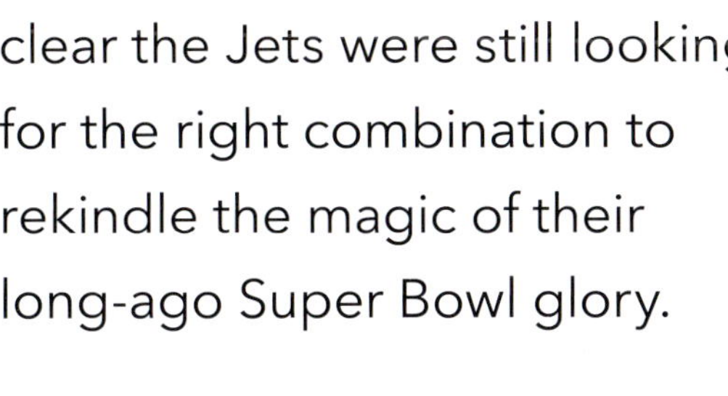

Quarterback Aaron Rodgers threw for 3,897 yards and 28 touchdowns in his first full season with the Jets.

TIMELINE

1960
The New York Titans are founded as part of the new AFL.

1963
The Titans are renamed the New York Jets after owner Sonny Werblin buys the team.

1965
The Jets sign quarterback Joe Namath to a record $427,000 contract.

1967
Namath throws for a record 4,007 yards.

1969
The Jets upset the Baltimore Colts 16–7 in Super Bowl III on January 12, backing up Namath's bold victory guarantee.

1981
The Jets reach the playoffs for the first time in 12 years.

Led by "the New York Sack Exchange," the Jets reach the AFC title game on January 23.

1983

1987

After finishing 10-6 during the regular season, the Jets lose in the divisional playoffs to the Cleveland Browns on January 3.

The Jets finish a franchise-worst 1-15.

1996

1998

The Jets win their first division title since the 1970 merger. The following January, they lose to the Denver Broncos in the playoffs.

The Jets reach the AFC title game but lose 30-17 to the Indianapolis Colts on January 24.

2010

2011

New York defeats the rival Patriots in the divisional round but falls short of the Super Bowl after losing 24-19 to the Pittsburgh Steelers in the AFC title game on January 23.

Jets cornerback Sauce Gardner and wide receiver Garrett Wilson become only the third teammates to both win Rookie of the Year.

2022

2024

The Jets miss the playoffs for the 14th consecutive season, the longest active streak in the NFL.

GLOSSARY

bankrupt–unable to pay debts.

blitz–when a linebacker or defensive back attacks the line of scrimmage to stop a run or sack the quarterback.

comeback–a big rally after falling behind.

commissioner–the chief executive of a sports league.

coordinator–an assistant coach who is in charge of the offense, defense, or special teams.

draft–a system that allows teams to acquire new players coming into a league.

franchise–an entire sports organization.

iconic–well known for excellence.

merger–joining one thing with another to create something new, such as a company, a team, or a league.

overtime–an extra period of play when the score is tied after regulation.

players' strike–a work stoppage due to a disagreement between players and their employers (teams) about things such as working conditions or wages.

postseason–another word for playoffs; the time after the end of the regular season when teams play to determine a champion.

resign–to leave a job.

rival–an opponent with whom a player or team has a fierce and ongoing competition.

rookie—a professional athlete in his or her first year of competition.

sack—a tackle of the quarterback behind the line of scrimmage before he can pass the ball.

tactic—a carefully planned action or strategy.

underdog—the person or team that is not expected to win.

veteran—someone who has played for many years.

ONLINE RESOURCES

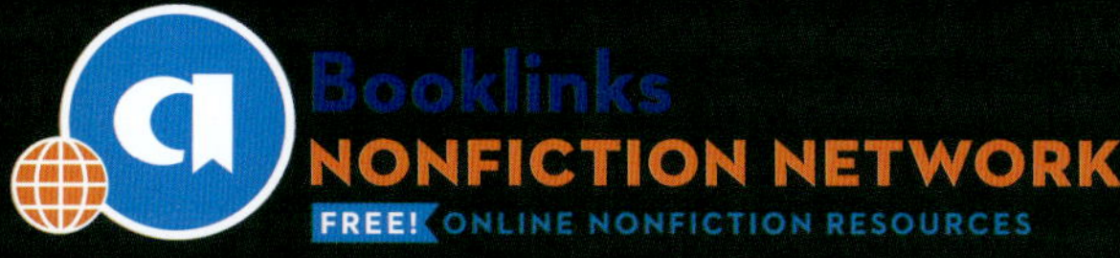

To learn more about the New York Jets, please visit **abdobooklinks.com** or scan this QR code. These links are routinely monitored and updated to provide the most current information available.

INDEX